THE LITTLE GUIDE TO
MESSI

Published in 2024 by OH!
An Imprint of Welbeck Non-Fiction Limited,
part of Welbeck Publishing Group.
Offices in London – 20 Mortimer Street, London W1T 3JW
and Sydney – Level 17, 207 Kent St, Sydney NSW 2000 Australia
www.welbeckpublishing.com

Disclaimer:
This publication may contain copyrighted material, the use of which has not been specifically authorised by the copyright owner. The material in this publication is made available in this book under the fair use and intended only for review, research and news reporting purposes only. The publisher is not associated with any names, football clubs or associations, trademarks, service marks and trade names referred to herein, which are the property of their respective owners and are used solely for identification purposes. This book is a publication of *OH! an Imprint of Welbeck Non-Fiction Limited* and has not been licensed, approved, sponsored, or endorsed by any person or entity.

A CIP catalogue record of this book is available from the British Library.

ISBN 978 1 80069 674 7

Printed in Dubai

10 9 8 7 6 5 4 3 2

THE LITTLE GUIDE TO
MESSI

Compiled and written by
DAVID CLAYTON

UNOFFICIAL AND UNAUTHORIZED

CONTENTS

Introduction

Lionel Messi is regarded as one of the greatest soccer players of all time–if not *the* greatest.

He is like no soccer player before or since. A maestro with the gift to do the seemingly impossible. A magician with vision and trickery far beyond that of his peers.

A phenomenon.

A humble and shy youngster from a working-class family in Rosario, Argentina, who became the most famous soccer player of all time, he was diagnosed with a growth hormone deficiency as an 11-year-old which required expensive treatment.

Though his father's insurance policy covered some of the payments, the talented youngster was left without the medication he needed. Aged 13, and with no other options, he was sent to Catalonia in Spain to stay with relatives and a trial with Barcelona was arranged.

Once Barça saw Messi play, they were so concerned he would be snapped up by a rival that a contract was hastily written by club officials on a napkin and Leo was officially a Barcelona player. The rest is history.

His incredible career has been mostly centred around his 21-year stay at the Camp Nou, where he is still revered as a soccer god. Barça's financial predicament meant the unthinkable finally happened in 2021 when Leo left for Paris Saint-Germain.

His popularity around the globe remains undiminished, adored by millions of soccer fans who put rivalries aside to salute this incredible player. He has won every major honour there is to win, including the coveted Ballon d'Or on a record seven occasions.

The one medal missing from his collection was that of a World Cup winner, but in December 2022 he inspired his nation to glory, finally lifting the trophy after scoring twice in the final against France.

Lional Messi is the Argentinian genius who has taken the beautiful game to unchartered levels during a glittering 21 year career–and now with a move to Miami he's certainly not finished yet!

CHAPTER 1

• • •

A STAR IS BORN

24 June 1987.

Nobody knew at the time, but a superstar had arrived and life for the Messi family would never be the same again...

“From the age of three,
I played every day – morning, afternoon
and night.”

LIONEL MESSI

gives an insight to how his path to stardom began

“I got given my first football when I was very young: three, maybe, or four. It was a present and from then on it was the only present I ever wanted, Christmas, birthday or whatever: a ball.”

LIONEL MESSI

recalls a pivotal moment in his young life as quoted on sport360.com, June 2015

"When I was four or five years old I was already playing with a ball, as soon as I started walking."

LIONEL MESSI

recalls how it all began, as quoted on getfootballnewsspain.com, May 2021

"At first, I used to collect them. I didn't want to take them out in the street in case they burst or got damaged. After a while, though, I started taking them outside and actually playing football with them!"

LIONEL MESSI

Messi's most treasured possessions – footballs – were initially placed on a pedestal and revered. As quoted on sport360.com, June 2015

“To be honest, I didn’t like studying and it was hard for me, but I always behaved well.”

LIONEL MESSI

admits his attention was elsewhere from an early age, as quoted on getfootballnewsspain.com, May 2021

“We lived in a nice, ordinary house in a neighbourhood in the south of the city called Barrio Las Heras. It’s still my barrio. We have the same house – although we’ve done it up since I was a boy – and I always go home to visit when I can and still see lots of the same friends.”

LIONEL MESSI

reflects on his humble beginnings and why they remain so important to him, as quoted on sport360.com, June 2015

"My family have guided me in my life, but in playing football? Sincerely, the truth is: no. I've always just done what seemed to come naturally. And haven't had to think about it."

LIONEL MESSI

admits he did what came naturally – despite the best intentions of his parents and siblings! As quoted on sport360.com, June 2015

24 June 1987

Known all around the world simply as Lionel Messi, he was born in Rosario, the largest city in the central Argentine province of Santa Fe, and named Luis Lionel Andrés Messi.

> "You can overcome anything, if – and if only – you love something enough."

LIONEL MESSI

Messi – perhaps referencing his own growth problems that threatened a career in football – shares advice that everyone can relate to

“Many years ago when I first started my career Maradona told me ‘to enjoy and play as you know’, and that’s stayed with me ever since and is the best advice I’ve been given.”

LIONEL MESSI

reveals how one Argentinian legend helped create another…

The Machine of ‘87

Growing up with a passion for sport, at the age of 6 Leo joined Newell’s Old Boys, the local Rosario club.

In the 6 years he played for them he scored almost 500 goals.

Almost unbeaten during those years, the youth team became known as “The Machine of ‘87”, named after the year of the players birth.

“You have to fight to achieve your dreams. You have to sacrifice and work hard for it.”

LIONEL MESSI

Advice any aspiring youngster should heed, as quoted in Verve Magazine, *2016*

“I’ve got a feeling that sometimes, when I was playing football in the street with my brother and his friends, they’d lose a game on purpose. They’d let me win because they knew that, if they didn’t, there’d be trouble.”

LIONEL MESSI

admits to being a sore loser from an early age, as quoted on sport360.com, June 2015

> "I was always the smallest kid, at school and in my teams."

LIONEL MESSI

If anyone has proved that size isn't everything in football and life, it is Lionel Messi

“I know how important it is to have a helping hand. In my childhood I had difficult times because of hormonal problems. If I hadn’t had support, I wouldn’t have been able to fulfil my dreams.”

LIONEL MESSI

always remembers those that helped him overcome his physical issues – notaby his parents, his doctors in Argentina and his doctor at FC Barcelona

“At first my parents gave me the injections from when I was eight years old until I learnt. It was a small needle. It did not hurt, it was something routine for me that I had to do and I did it with normality.”

LIONEL MESSI

explains how taking a growth hormone injection became part of his everyday life for several years, as quoted on mirror.co.uk, 2018

“When you saw him you would think: this kid can’t play ball… he’s too fragile, too small. But immediately you’d realise that he was born different, that he was a phenomenon and that he was going to be something impressive.”

ADRIÁN CORIA,

the Newell’s Old Boys youth coach, sharing his first impression of the 12-year-old Messi

“I don’t know, I’ve liked football since I was a kid and I’ve always dreamt of becoming a professional footballer, I never thought of any other job.”

LIONEL MESSI

Leo’s one-track mind would pay off handsomely…

“Football has been my life since I was a kid. My style remains the same, I love every single minute I get on the pitch. I know I have a great responsibility, and that there are objectives to accomplish, but I try to have fun too, because that’s what I love to do.”

LIONEL MESSI

Leo’s lifelong love affair with the game is one of the reasons he achieved greatness

“I never had any problems with my height.”

LIONEL MESSI

Pint-sized and lightly built he may have been but courage and ability more than made up for anything he lacked in physicality

“You have got to love the game.”

LIONEL MESSI

Simple advice from the master…

"I made sacrifices leaving Argentina, leaving my family to begin a new life. I changed my friends, my people. Everything. But everything I did, I did for soccer, to achieve my dream."

LIONEL MESSI

reflects on leaving Argentina, his family, and friends in order to pursue his career.

Celebration

Messi has a trademark celebration after scoring a goal.

He points towards the sky with both arms, to dedicate his goals to his grandmother, whom he loved immensely.

“In my entire life I have never seen a player of such quality and personality at such a young age, particularly wearing the ‘heavy’ shirt of one of the world’s great clubs.”

FABIO CAPELLO,

then managing Juventus, praises the 18-year-old Messi following the Joan Gamper trophy game in August 2005

“I would tell him that something extraordinary is on the way, something he can’t imagine. I’d tell him that his career will have a beautiful path, with hard moments he will have to overcome, but he should never quit, because he will be rewarded, and in the end, it will be just like a movie with a happy ending.”

LIONEL MESSI

When asked what 35-year-old Lionel would say to his teenage self in an interview with Argentine radio host Andy Kusnetzoff, as quoted in the Buenos Aires Herald, *April 2023*

Spain

As a resident of Spain since the age of 13, Messi has held dual nationality and is qualified to play for Spain.

He was invited to play for the Spanish Under-20 side in 2004 but turned down the opportunity and instead led Argentina to victory in the FIFA Youth Championship a year later.

CHAPTER 2

• • •

INSPIRATIONAL GENIUS

Whether it's because of what he does on the pitch, his humble nature, or the things he says, Lionel Messi is an inspiration to millions upon millions around the world...

“Every year I try to grow as a player and not get stuck in a rut. I try to improve my game in every way possible.”

LIONEL MESSI

Words to inspire any youngster and ones Leo has kept as his mantra from his first steps in football with Newell's Old Boys

“I’m happy with a ball at my feet. My motivation comes from playing the game I love.”

LIONEL MESSI

as quoted in Verve Magazine, *2016*

“I try to use pressure to help me in every game. Pressure helps me do things to the best of my ability. I like it. I don’t feel pressure; quite the contrary, because I always enjoy what I’m doing and that’s playing football.”

LIONEL MESSI

Like so many artists, he needs demands placing on his shoulders to get the very best out of himself

“The day you think there is no improvements to be made is a sad one for any player.”

LIONEL MESSI

Wise words, especially for younger players who have praise lavished on them quickly, as quoted in Verve Magazine, *2016*

> “My ambition is always to get better and better.”

LIONEL MESSI

Good news for Leo. Bad news for the opposition!

Words spoken at a young age and adopted through his career, as quoted on spanishmama.com, May 2022

“The best decisions aren’t made with your mind, but with your instincts.”

LIONEL MESSI

Hard to argue with anything Leo says given his achievements!

As quoted on kidadl.com, 2021

“I still have a lot of room for improvement. For example, I want to shoot equally well with both feet.”

LIONEL MESSI

Now that would be frightening…

“Whether it’s a friendly match, or for points, or a final, or any game – I play the same. I’m always trying to be my best, first for my team, for myself, for the fans, and to try and win.”

LIONEL MESSI

Born winners know no other way…

Religion

Messi is a devout Roman Catholic.

He met with Pope Francis at the Vatican in 2013, which he has said was one of the greatest days of his life.

“I like to score goals, but I also like to have friends among the people I have played with.”

LIONEL MESSI

As the old saying goes, there is no ‘I’ in T E A M

“Without the help of my teammates I would be nothing. I wouldn’t win titles, honours, nothing.”

LIONEL MESSI

It’s fair to say that Leo’s team-mates would say that without him, they wouldn’t have won so many titles and trophies!

“I am a normal person. I have the same life as any human being. When I finish playing, doing my work, I have my family, my friends, and I live like any other person.”

LIONEL MESSI

Humbleness, and humility are not attributes Leo struggles with…

“Every time I start a year, I start with the objective of trying to achieve everything, without comparing it to how I’ve done in other seasons.”

LIONEL MESSI

A good way of keeping the pressure off one’s shoulders…

“Sometimes, you have to accept you can’t win all the time.”

LIONEL MESSI

Sound advice – though Leo is a self-confessed bad loser!

Charity

Messi does not only show greatness on the pitch but also off the pitch. He is the founder of the Leo Messi Foundation, an organisation that aims to give children the best opportunities for education and healthcare.

His foundation also helps to pay for medical treatment, transportation and recuperation for children diagnosed with major medical problems.

“Before if I lost or did something wrong I didn’t talk to anyone for three or four days until it passed. Now, I come home after a game, I see my son, and everything is alright.”

LIONEL MESSI

Age has certainly mellowed his reaction to losing, though it is more about his son helping to put things into perspective in this instance...

“When the year starts the objective is to win it all with the team, personal records are secondary.”

LIONEL MESSI

With Leo in the side, those objectives are successfully met, more often than not, as quoted on kidadl.com, 2021

“Being a bit famous now gives me the opportunity to help people who really need it, especially children.”

LIONEL MESSI

The slightly famous Leo putting his celebrity to great use…

“Something deep in my character allows me to take the hits and get on with trying to win.”

LIONEL MESSI

He's been subjected to plenty of hits, fouls and rash tackles in his career, but, like Diego Maradona, stopping him in full flow is a near impossibility…

“My style of play has always been the same. I never tried to develop a specific style. From very young I just played this way.”

LIONEL MESSI

A unique style and one that definitely works!

"I'm always proudest whenever I've been part of a trophy-winning team. Lifting a title makes me feel so happy because it's what I want to do in football: be successful."

LIONEL MESSI

A team player before all else…

“I would pass onto any young player to enjoy your football, play your football as you want to play the game, try and enjoy it and make the most of it.”

LIONEL MESSI

shares the secrets of his incredible successes – play with a smile and with freedom

“I’m lucky to be part of a team who help to make me look good, and they deserve as much of the credit for my success as I do for the hard work we have all put in on the training ground.”

LIONEL MESSI

Humble to a fault – Leo would rather spread the praise around his teammates than hog the limelight

> “Goals are only important if they win games.”

LIONEL MESSI

dismisses talk of which is his favourite goal – though his percentage of winning goals is extremely high, as quoted on kidadl.com, 2021

"I am more worried about being a good person than being the best football player in the world."

LIONEL MESSI

A statement that pretty much sums up the best footballer in the world and his simplistic outlook on life, as quoted on kidadl.com, 2021

“Motivation is not something I struggle with. I love playing football, I love being in training.”

LIONEL MESSI

Words any manager would love to hear from his star player, as quoted on kidadl.com, 2021

"There are more important things in life than winning or losing a game."

LIONEL MESSI

It is, indeed, only a game after all… not life and death, as quoted in Verve Magazine*, 2016*

"There's nothing more satisfying than seeing a happy and smiling child. I always help in any way I can, even if it's just by signing an autograph. A child's smile is worth more than all the money in the world."

LIONEL MESSI

Leo has been making kids around the globe happy for many years, as quoted on kidadl.com, 2021

“Money is not a motivating factor. Money doesn’t thrill me or make me play better because there are benefits to being wealthy… If I wasn’t paid to be a professional footballer I would willingly play for nothing.”

LIONEL MESSI

Leo’s love of the game shines through – but his agent might advise against saying this ahead of any contract negotiations! As quoted in Verve Magazine, *2016*

"I fell a lot of times, but I always decided to get up and try again. It happened many times with Barcelona and more with Argentina. It was a message to my children and the young boys who follow me, who are fighting for their dreams."

LIONEL MESSI

The message from Leo is that great talents are always targeted – it is the reaction of the target that defines them as a person and a footballer. As quoted on Argentine journalist Roy Nemer's Twitter page, November 2021

CHAPTER 3

• • •

BARÇA BRILLIANCE

No matter what Lionel Messi achieves in his career or who he plays for, one club – Barcelona – will forever be his true footballing love...

Barcelona

In 2000, after watching Leo Messi play in just one match, former Barcelona player and coach Carles Rexach decided to sign him on the spot, and to ensure he didn't sign for anyone else, he wrote a contract onto a paper napkin which Messi duly signed!

“Barcelona is my home and I hope that I stay here for many years.”

LIONEL MESSI

He may have had to leave to live in Paris, but he will no doubt return to Catalonia at some stage in the future

“Personally and in terms of football, coming to Barcelona was an extraordinary change. When I was in Argentina, I only ran but I hardly played with the ball.”

LIONEL MESSI

Leo's seismic life change was not only off the pitch but on it, too.

As quoted on 90min.com, November 2022

“I had a very difficult year. I was six months without being able to play and when I came back, I was injured again. One day, my father asked me if I wanted to go back. I said ‘no’. I had done the most difficult part, which was adapting.”

LIONEL MESSI

It might have all been different had Leo not had the determination to succeed and follow his dreams. As quoted on 90min.com, November 2022

“Ronaldinho, Deco, [Thiago] Motta, Sylvinho, Xavi, [Carles] Puyol…they all made me feel like one of them from the start. The way they treated me was great. It’s not easy to come into a dressing room like that and be able to integrate normally.”

LIONEL MESSI

A future superstar is greeted by superstars, as quoted on 90min.com, November 2022

“At Barça we trained every day with the ball. I hardly even took a step running without a ball at my feet.”

LIONEL MESSI

The Catalans' purist ways were very much to the liking of Leo

2004-05

In the 2004-05 season Messi, then 17, became the youngest official player and goal scorer in the Spanish La Liga.

He made his debut against Espanyol in October 2004 aged 17 years and 322 days old. His goal against Albacete in May 2005 also made him Barcelona's youngest scorer ever at the time.

“The Barcelona youth program is one of the best in the world. As a kid, they teach you not to play to win, but to grow in ability as a player.”

LIONEL MESSI

Player and club were well-suited!

“The Guardiola era was an extraordinary period. Everything happened. Guardiola comes in, with what he taught us and made us grow as a team. He found a generation of players that was unique. It was impressive.”

LIONEL MESSI

recalls perhaps his perfect manager's early days as boss, as quoted on @BarçaUniversal Twitter account, November 2022

“I always liked having the ball at my feet. I loved having Xavi, Iniesta, and Busquets next to me. It was all so much easier.”

LIONEL MESSI

Barça's style allowed Leo to focus on wreaking havoc with his skills and instincts, as quoted on 90mins.com, November 2022

“With Guardiola, we made things so easy, and it was so natural that we didn’t realise what we were doing. As time goes by, you realise it was unique what we achieved.”

LIONEL MESSI

reflects on perhaps the happiest times of his career in a devastating Barça side with a manager who changed the face of football. As quoted on 90mins.com, November 2022

“Guardiola is the best coach, I have no doubt. He is special. He prepared the games like nobody else. He knew everything. I regret not having enjoyed the Guardiola era more, not having enjoyed it more with him.”

LIONEL MESSI

More from Messi on his favourite coach and the methods he employed, as quoted on 90min.com, November 2022

“Guardiola did football a lot of harm because he made it look so easy and so simple that everyone wanted to copy him.”

LIONEL MESSI

Leo says it’s all Pep Guardiola’s fault! As quoted on ESPN.com, November 2022

“Without a doubt. He has something special, above all how he watched and prepared for matches and how he communicates, because of how he transmitted it to you.”

LIONEL MESSI

More Leo praise for Pep Guardiola, as quoted on ESPN.com, November 2022

“Pep is the best coach I’ve ever had. Everything he planned always ended up happening.”

LIONEL MESSI

More praise for his former gaffer – and the feeling is mutual!

As quoted in FourFourTwo, *November 2022*

UNICEF

Messi was named a UNICEF Goodwill ambassador in 2010 after first being involved with the charity in 2004.

Barcelona FC has close links to the charity – which supports children and disadvantaged youngsters in more than 190 countries, and Messi has been integral in multiple charitable efforts in the past decade.

"It doesn't matter if I am better than Cristiano Ronaldo, all that matters is that Barcelona are better than Madrid."

LIONEL MESSI

explains his thinking and priorities to look at the bigger picture, as quoted on @BarçaWorldwide Twitter account, 2018

“I struggled in the dressing room but once I got on the pitch the problems were over. I missed going out on the street and playing like I used to do it in Argentina.”

LIONEL MESSI

reflects on the early days at Barça, as quoted on 90min.com, November 2022

“I start early, and I stay late, day after day, year after year, it took me 17 years and 114 days to become an overnight success.”

LIONEL MESSI

reacting on Twitter to the claims he was an overnight success for Barcelona not long after his senior debut, August 2018

“It's crazy to say that after three games [without a goal] I was in crisis. I do not care whether I score or not, what matters is that the team win and continue to do so.”

LIONEL MESSI

responds to questions about his three-game goal 'drought' at Barcelona, October 2011

“It’s not so easy for us when we play teams who have a different mindset, like Chelsea or Inter Milan, because they have the intention of trying to stop us rather than playing a game that is more attractive for the spectators to enjoy.”

LIONEL MESSI

is not a fan of teams who “park the bus” as the saying goes

“I don’t need the best hairstyle or the best body. Just give me a ball at my feet and I’ll show you what I can do.”

LIONEL MESSI

has a little dig at some of today’s over-pampered footballers who spend as much time on their looks as they do practicing and playing

2012

Lionel Messi scored an incredible 91 goals in the calendar year of 2012, thus beating Gerd Müller's record of 85 goals scored in 1972 that had stood for 40 years.

“We are at a good level. Our secret is that we play the same way against each opponent.”

LIONEL MESSI

Leo saves opposition managers the problem of watching Barcelona at their peak!

“Without me, Barcelona would be the same, without Barcelona I would be nothing.”

LIONEL MESSI

A statement that many believe to be not quite true!

As quoted on sportbible.com, April 2019

"I told the club, including the president, that I wanted to go. I've been telling him that all year. I believed that the club needed more young players, new players and I thought my time in Barcelona was over. I felt very sorry because I always said that I wanted to finish my career here."

LIONEL MESSI

Leo explaining why he told Barça that he wanted to leave, resulting in a predictable outcry from millions of Barça fans. As quoted on goal.com in an interview with Rubén Uría, 4 September 2020

“[The decision to leave] did not come because of the Champions League result against Bayern Munich [Barça lost at home 8-2]. No, I had been thinking about the decision for a long time. I told the president and, well, the president always said that at the end of the season I could decide if I wanted to go or if I wanted to stay and in the end he did not keep his word.”

LIONEL MESSI

as quoted on goal.com in an interview with Rubén Uría, 4 September 2020

"Every year I could have left and earned more money than at Barcelona. I always said that this was my home, and it was what I felt and feel. To decide there was somewhere better than here was difficult. I felt that I needed a change and new goals, new things."

LIONEL MESSI

as quoted on goal.com in an interview with Rubén Uría, 4 September 2020

“There is a new coach and new ideas. That’s good, but then we have to see how the team responds and whether or not it will compete at the top level. What I can say is that I’m staying and I’m going to give my best for Barcelona.”

LIONEL MESSI

reaffirms that he has decided to stay at the Camp Nou, as quoted on goal.com in an interview with Rubén Uría, 4 September 2020

"I heard people talking about Andrés virtually from the moment I arrived at Barcelona. I didn't meet him at La Masia. I would go there to eat but we rarely crossed paths because I was preparing for my Bachillerato exams at the time. There are three years between us… he has always been the same, as a person and a player."

LIONEL MESSI

talks about Barça teammate Andrés Iniesta and their closeness on the pitch, if not off it, as quoted on skysports.com, April 2010

“I always picture him with the ball at his feet. That’s the way I have got used to seeing him. He does everything well, with simplicity. At times, it may look like he’s not doing anything, but in fact he’s doing it all. Everything is different with Andrés. The hardest thing to do in football is to make it look like everything is easy, effortless, and that’s Andrés.”

LIONEL MESSI

on Andrés Iniesta, as quoted on besoccer.com, 2017

“We’re more similar in the fact that we don’t talk much. He sits in one corner, I sit in another. But we cross paths, we connect; with just a look we understand each other. We don’t need more than that.”

LIONEL MESSI

on Andrés Iniesta, as quoted on besoccer.com, 2017

“Congratulations on your historic record, Lionel. But above all, congratulations on your beautiful career at Barcelona. Stories like ours, of loving the same club for so long, unfortunately will be increasingly rare in football. I admire you very much, Leo Messi.”

PELÉ

congratulates Messi after he overtook his record in scoring the most goals for one club, as seen in Sports Illustrated, *22 December 2020*

El Clasico

Nobody has scored more goals or assisted goals in the El Clasico game between Barcelona and Real Madrid than Lionel Messi, who has scored 26 times and created 14 more for teammates.

“I will not, nor waste any time.”

LIONEL MESSI

Leo's blunt response to suggestions Real Madrid were preparing an offer to pair him with Cristiano Ronaldo in 2013 – as recounted by the Daily Express*, February 2022*

"I know what Real Madrid is, I've lived it for many years, all my life, up close."

LIONEL MESSI

reacts to PSG's failure to win the 2022 Champions League and Real Madrid's continued success in the competition, as quoted on managingmadrid.com, May 2022

“Barcelona is my life, they have brought me to where I am today, I could not leave, I don’t want to leave. My heart stays with Barcelona.”

LIONEL MESSI

after deciding to stay at the Camp Nou, as quoted on goal.com, September 2020

"I've been here so many years, my entire life since I was 13. After 21 years I'm leaving with my wife, with my three little Catalan-Argentine kids and I can't tell you everything we've lived in this city and I can't say that in a few years we won't come back, because this is our home, and I promised my children that."

LIONEL MESSI

An emotional Leo speaking at his farewell press conference, 8 August 2021

“So many beautiful things have happened – also some bad things – but all of this helped me to grow, helped me to improve, and made me the person that I am today. I gave everything for this club, for this shirt, from the first day I arrived until the very last.”

LIONEL MESSI

speaks from the heart at his farewell press conference, 8 August 2021

“I leave this club now without seeing the fans for over a year and a half. If I’d have imagined it, I’d have imagined the Camp Nou full, being close to people and being able to say goodbye properly. But it has to be this way.”

LIONEL MESSI

More from a heartbroken Leo at his farewell press conference, 8 August 2021

Barça 2004-21

Senior team honours

La Liga:

2004-05, 2005-06, 2008-09, 2009-10, 2010-11, 2012-13, 2014-15, 2015-16, 2017-18, 2018-19

Copa del Rey:

2008-09, 2011-12, 2014-15, 2015-16, 2016-17, 2017-18, 2020-21

Supercopa de España:

2005, 2006, 2009, 2010, 2011, 2013, 2016, 2018

UEFA Champions League:
2005-06, 2008-09, 2010-11, 2014-15

UEFA Super Cup:
2009, 2011, 2015

FIFA Club World Cup:
2009, 2011, 2015

“When I finish my career,
I will return to live in Barcelona,
it's my home.”

LIONEL MESSI

Leo's future intentions are clear, as quoted on ole.com, February 2023

Hat-tricks

Leo has scored 36 La Liga hat-tricks for Barça – a club and league record.

As of March 2023 he had scored 57 hat-tricks in his career, in all competitions for club and country. That's a lot of match-balls to keep in your cabinet!

CHAPTER 4

• • •

THE WORLD AT HIS FEET

The great and the good from the world of sport have their say on this exceptional footballer...

“I don’t know if you will be better than Maradona, but you will be taller.”

DIEGO SCHWARZTEIN

Messi’s endocrinologist makes a promise to him during his growth treatment, as quoted on goal.com, December 2015

“There is only one Messi.”

PEP GUARDIOLA

The Manchester City manager, one of Messi's biggest fans, ahead of City's Champions League clash with the Catalan giants, 2018

"Who is the Best Player in the World?
Leo Messi.
Who is the Best Player Ever?
Leo Messi."

ARSÈNE WENGER

The former Arsenal boss reveals he is an admirer of Leo!
As quoted on givemesport.com, June 2022

“Don’t write about him, don’t try to describe him. Just watch him.”

PEP GUARDIOLA

Pep advises journalists to set down their pens, close their laptops and just watch an artist at work instead of attempting to put what he does into words… 2018

"Messi or Cristiano –
Speed? Cristiano. Shot? Cristiano.
Dribbling? Messi.
Intelligence? Messi. Talent? Messi.
Winner is Messi!"

PEP GUARDIOLA

The Manchester City boss does a quick breakdown of why Messi edges Christiano Ronaldo 3-2 when asked who he rated the best in the world, 2018

"He's a great player, but the only relationship I have with him is a professional one. I do respect him a lot as a professional football player. Messi's left foot is very good – I would like to have that."

CRISTIANO RONALDO

The Portuguese star confirms Leo wasn't top of his list to come around for tea and biscuits – though he would like to relieve him of his left foot!

As quoted on footiecentral.com, 2016

“There’s no kid who doesn’t have your team flannel, no matter if it’s a fake, real or a made up one. Truly, you made your mark in everyone’s life. And that, to me, is beyond winning any World Cup…

No one can take that from you, and this is my gratitude, for the amount of happiness you bring to a lot of people. ”

SOFIA MARTINEZ

Television Publica reporter Sofia Martinez swerves off piste and takes the opportunity to thank Leo on behalf of all Argentinians during a TV interview, as quoted on mirror.com, December 2022

"For the world of football, Messi is a treasure because he is a role model for children around the world… Messi will be the player to win the most Ballon d'Ors in history. He will win five, six, seven. He is incomparable. He's in a different league."

JOHAN CRUYFF

The greatest Dutch footballer ever, and one of the best players the world has ever seen, correctly predicts Messi's future, as quoted on givemesport.com, June 2022

“Every time he plays, Leo Messi reminds me more of Maradona, both left-footed and short, Messi is the best player in the world. For us it is not a surprise. Since he began to come and train with us, we knew we would go down this path. Someday I will explain that I was at the birth of one of the footballing greats: Leo Messi.”

RONALDINHO

Messi's boyhood idol gives his opinion on his biggest fan, as quoted on Footie Central's 100 Best Lionel Messi Quotes, 2016

"Messi is a joke.
For me the best ever."

WAYNE ROONEY

The former England and Manchester United star praises Leo in his own, unique style, as quoted on givemesport.com, June 2022

“Messi, he’s exceptional. When you watch him, you feel there’s a child inside him and he is making some childhood dream come true. He’s a Great Player, not only for today but also for tomorrow.”

ERIC CANTONA

A typically expressive, poetic description of the Argentina star from the French maverick, as quoted on givemesport.com, June 2022

"I am also amazed with Messi, what he is doing is very good. He contributes a lot of very good things for the team. He is an individualist, but he always plays for the team. He covers well at the back, is organized, and finishes well with both feet. He is mischievous and is a very intelligent player. He applies pressure just where the pressure is needed."

ALFREDO DI STÉFANO

High praise indeed from the ex-Real Madrid and Argentina legend who sadly passed away in 2014. As quoted on 90min.com, January 2021

“Messi is a once in a generation player. It’s unlikely that any human being will repeat his numbers.”

GIANLUIGI BUFFON

Italy goalkeeper Buffon makes a salient point regarding Messi’s stats, as quoted on givemesport.com, June 2022

"My record stood for 40 years and now the best player in the world has broken it. I'm happy for him. Messi is fantastic. An incredible player, a giant. And such a nice and modest guy. Only one defect: he doesn't play at Bayern!"

GERD MÜLLER

The West German goal-machine – who netted 654 goals in 716 career appearances at club level – moves aside for Leo after he surpasses his 85 goals in a calendar year, as quoted in The Independent, *2012*

“Messi is the best player on the planet, and he keeps on improving at Barça, now the best team in the world. What Messi does on and off the pitch is an inspiration for children who dream of becoming a footballer.”

NOVAK DJOKOVIC

Serbian tennis star Novak Djokovic shares his thoughts on a different sporting champion… as quoted on factpros.com, 2016

“Messi is the best. There must be life out there somewhere, on some other planet. Because he is too good, and we are just too bad for him.”

JÜRGEN KLOPP

The Liverpool boss suggest Leo might have origins outside our galaxy…

"Messi does not need his right foot. He only uses the left and he's still the best in the world. Imagine if he also used his right foot, then we would have serious problems."

ZLATAN IBRAHIMOVIĆ

Zlatan – not one for giving out praise to others as a rule – salutes the Argentine genius, and makes a good point! As quoted on givemesport.com, June 2022

“I have seen the player who will inherit my place in Argentine football and his name is Messi. Messi is a genius.”

DIEGO MARADONA

hailing the 18-year-old Messi as his successor in February 2006

“Although he may not be human, it’s good that Messi still thinks he is.”

JAVIER MASCHERANO

Compatriot Mascherano suggests that Leo may not be of this planet!

As quoted on @WeAreMessi Twitter account, June 2020

“He’s well above anything else I’ve ever seen. He’s an alien.”

CARLES PUYOL

And yet more accusations that Leo may be of extra-terrestrial origin!
As quoted on Eurosport’s Best Ever Messi Quotes, February 2016

"It's been an absolute privilege to watch Messi for nearly 2 decades. Moment after moment of spellbinding, breathtakingly joyous football. A gift from the footballing Gods. So pleased that he's lifted the ultimate prize in our sport. Gracias y felicidades campeón."

GARY LINEKER

England legend and Match of the Day *anchor Gary Lineker is effusive with his praise as Leo lifts the World Cup, as quoted on @GaryLineker Twitter account, December 2022*

“Without supporting Argentina when Messi lifted the trophy I was moved to tears. For the emotion of seeing someone so great achieve what he missed after suffering so much for it.”

RAFAEL NADAL

Tennis legend and Spaniard Rafael Nadal relates to Leo's achievement after a long wait, as quoted on mirror.co.uk, December 2022

“I think Leo Messi. He is a skilled player, gives assists, passes, scores, dribbles well. If we were in a team together, the opponents would have to worry about two players, not just one. Today Messi is the most complete player.”

PELÉ

Pelé responds to the question of who he would most like to play alongside from the modern game, as quoted on Bleacher Report*, 2019*

“Everything he represents is incredible – not just for us, his team-mates, but for the club and everyone who loves football. I think everyone loves Leo, not just Barça fans. I love everything he does.”

IVAN RAKITIĆ

Former Barça team-mate Ivan Rakitić shares the love, as quoted on Eurosport, April 2016

"No words for you, Messi. You deserved to be World Champion before, but God knows all things and will crown you this Sunday, you deserve this title for the person you are and for the wonderful football you have always played. Hats off to you. God bless you."

RIVALDO

Former Brazil star sends Messi a message ahead of the World Cup final, as quoted on mirror.co.uk, December 2022

Ballon d'or

Messi won the 2009 Ballon d'or, beating Cristiano Ronaldo by collecting 473 of the votes, 240 more than Ronaldo's 233.

The largest margin ever!

“He is always going forwards. He never passes the ball backwards or sideways. He has only one idea, to run towards the goal. So as a football fan, just enjoy the show.”

ZINEDINE ZIDANE

From one world great to another – Zidane pinpoints Leo's highly effective methods, as quoted on givemesport.com, June 2022

CHAPTER 5

• • •

DON'T CRY FOR ME ARGENTINA

Fiercely patriotic, Lionel Messi might have lived outside of Argentina more than he has lived in it – but blood runs blue and white, with his love of his country never far from the surface…

“Argentina is my country, my family, my way of expressing myself. I would trade all of my records for the World Cup trophy.”

LIONEL MESSI

No need, Leo… as quoted on @MessiQuote Twitter account, 2014

Gold

Lionel won his first major honour with Argentina – an Olympic gold medal at the 2008 games in Beijing after beating Nigeria 1-0 in the final.

2006

Messi was sent on for his World Cup debut in the 76th minute against Serbia and Montenegro at Germany 2006.

Within three minutes he'd set up Hernán Crespo to score and ten minutes later he slotted home to seal a 6-0 victory – Argentina's joint-biggest in the competition.

“For me the national team is over. I've done all I can, it hurts not to be a champion. It's been four finals, it's not meant for me. I tried. It was the thing I wanted most, but I couldn't get it, so I think it's over.”

LIONEL MESSI

Leo can't hide his bitter disappointment after the 4-2 Copa America defeat to Chile, as quoted on barçablaugranes.com, June 2016

“It’s very difficult, but the decision has been made. I won’t try it any longer and on this there will be no going back.”

LIONEL MESSI

Leo, thankfully, would reverse this decision… as quoted on CBS Soccer, *June 2016*

"It hurts me like nobody else, I leave without being able to win a title."

LIONEL MESSI

The end was nigh, or so it seemed at the time, as quoted on CBS Soccer, *June 2016*

Argentina

As of 31 March 2023, Messi had played 174 times for Argentina, scoring 102 goals.

He made his international debut in August 2005 against Hungary coming on as a substitute at 63 minutes – and was sent off two minutes later!

"There are no excuses. We are going to be more united than ever. This group is strong, and they have shown it. It is a situation that we did not have to go through in a long time."

LIONEL MESSI

reacts after Argentina's shock defeat to Saudi Arabia at the 2022 World Cup, as quoted on talksport.com, November 2022

"Now we have to show that this is a real group. It's a very hard blow for everyone, we didn't expect to start like this."

LIONEL MESSI

More reaction after Argentina's shock defeat to Saudi Arabia at the 2022 World Cup, as quoted on talksport.com, November 2022

"Things happen for a reason. We have to prepare for what's coming, we have to win or win, and it depends on us."

LIONEL MESSI

Only one message after Argentina's shock defeat to Saudi Arabia at the 2022 World Cup, as quoted on talksport.com, November 2022

"I hope the people in Argentina enjoy themselves and what we are doing. They shouldn't doubt we are giving absolutely everything."

LIONEL MESSI

The Albiceleste No.10 sends a message back home ahead of the World Cup final, as quoted in The National, *December 2022*

"CHAMPIONS OF THE WORLD!!!!!!!
So many times I dreamed it, so much I wanted it that I still don't fall, I can't believe it."

LIONEL MESSI

After finally winning the World Cup, Leo posts on his official Instagram page, and the 75m likes he receives almost break the internet!

18 December 2022

"Thank you so much to my family, to all who support me and also to all who believed in us. We prove once again that Argentinians when we fight together and united we are able to achieve what we aim."

LIONEL MESSI

posts more on his official Instagram page post-World Cup, 18 December 2022

"I achieved everything with the national team as I always dreamed. I got everything in my career, individually. It was about closing my career in a unique way."

LIONEL MESSI

expresses his delight as his boyhood dream finally comes true, as quoted on FIFA.com, December 2022

“I never imagined that all this was going to happen to me when I started and getting to this moment was the best. I have no complaints and I can’t ask for more.”

LIONEL MESSI

shares his joy with the world, as quoted on FIFA.com, December 2022

“We won the Copa America [in 2021] and the World Cup, there's nothing left.”

LIONEL MESSI

The maestro hints at retirement? As quoted on Goal.com, January 2023

2022

Lionel Messi became the first player to win five Man of the Match awards at the 2022 World Cup. Aged 35. Incredible.

"I think if I had to choose the moment, it would have been this one. It's at the end of my career, closing a cycle."

LIONEL MESSI

More hints that his international career might have reached a natural conclusion…? As quoted on punditfeed.com, January 2023

“I knew God would bring this gift to me, I had the feeling that this World Cup was the one.”

LIONEL MESSI

reacts after winning the World Cup, as quoted on Mail Online, *18 December 2022*

"It took so long, but here it is. We suffered a lot, but we managed to do it. Can't wait to be in Argentina to witness the insanity of this."

LIONEL MESSI

More reaction after winning the World Cup, as quoted on Mail Online, *18 December 2022*

“The World Cup was calling me.
It said to me ‘Here I am, come and grab me,
now you can touch me!’”

LIONEL MESSI

recalls the moments before he lifted the World Cup, as quoted on marca.com, 30 January 2023

"I saw it shining there, it stood out in that beautiful stadium, and I didn't think about it, I went to kiss it because I passed by it. I needed it."

LIONEL MESSI

recalls the moment he kissed the trophy before he lifted it, as quoted on marca.com, 30 January 2023

"I would have liked Diego to give me the cup, or at least to see all this, to see Argentina as world champions, with everything he wanted and how he loved the national team."

LIONEL MESSI

One wish even Leo couldn't be granted, as quoted on FIFA.com, December 2022

“I'm not retiring from the national team. I want to continue playing as champion.”

LIONEL MESSI

reacts after winning the World Cup, as quoted on Mail Online, *December 2022*

Winner

Messi was offered the chance to play for the Spanish national team, but he turned it down and decided to wait on Argentina's call-up.

Either way he would have ended up a World Cup winner!

"We did it!!!
LET'S GO ARGENTINA DAMN!!!!!
We're seeing each other
very soon..."

LIONEL MESSI

posts on his official Instagram page ahead of the Argentina squad's homecoming, December 2022

CHAPTER 6

• • •

THE GREATEST SHOWMAN

Magician, visionary, and possibly the world's Greatest Showman… the one and only Lionel Messi.

“One of the Arsenal players came up to me afterwards and said it had been an honour to be on the same pitch as me. I thought, My God, that is a great thing to say when your team has just lost.”

LIONEL MESSI

After his four-goal super show against Arsenal, Leo is impressed by the English sportsmanship, as quoted in themirror.co.uk, 2010

La Pulga

Lionel Messi is nicknamed “La Pulga Atomica” which means “The Atomic Flea” due to his fast, deadly, tricky style of play and the fact that he pops up here, there and everywhere!

“Like I’ve said many times before, I’m always more likely to remember goals for their importance rather than if they’re beautiful or not. Goals scored in finals, for example.”

LIONEL MESSI

That still leaves a lot of goals to remember!

"I don't consider myself the best, I think I'm just another player. On the pitch, we are all the same when the game begins."

LIONEL MESSI,

the modest genius, as quoted on @Messi Quote, June 2018

“Thank you very much to my teammates and to all the people in the club for the welcome they gave me. We are back and looking forward to continuing to meet the objectives of this season, now with PSG.”

LIONEL MESSI

posts a message on his Instagram page on his return to PSG after the World Cup, January 2023

“I have fun like a child in the street. When the day comes when I’m not enjoying it, I will leave football.”

LIONEL MESSI

taps into his childhood love of the game – and reveals what will happen if he ever loses it

Ballon d'Or

Lionel Messi has won the coveted Ballon d'Or award on no less than seven occasions – in 2009, 2010, 2011, 2012, 2015, 2019 and 2021.

The prize is given to the world's top male player and Leo won them all with Barcelona.

“I always try to create danger.”

LIONEL MESSI

explains what his aims and methods are each time he plays…

as quoted in the New York Times, *May 2011*

"I don't look at records, that's not why I'm playing the game. Goals, of course. Every player in my position wants to score goals. But most of all, trophies. My target is always to win trophies, and that will always be my motivation, to win things. Nothing feels better than doing that as a team."

LIONEL MESSI

He's not in this for self-promotion, that's for sure... as quoted on thehindu.com, 2015

"In football as in watchmaking, talent and elegance mean nothing without rigour and precision."

LIONEL MESSI

attempts to convey his art by comparing it to another, as quoted on @TeamMessi Twitter account, March 2014

"And now, I think what people there understand is that this is a team game, and that I try to play the same way there, for Argentina as I do in Barcelona, and always do the best I can."

LIONEL MESSI

speaking ahead of the 2014 World Cup final… surely nobody could ever doubt he had never tried his best or given his all for club and country. As quoted on reuters.com, July 2014

"I never think about the play or visualize anything. I do what comes to me at that moment. Instinct. It has always been that way."

LIONEL MESSI

He has always played on instinct; it has got him to where he is today, and he trusts it completely. As quoted on azquotes.com

“I had said I didn’t mind which shirt I played in, but coming from Diego, Number 10 is very special.”

LIONEL MESSI

One icon follows in the footsteps of another and, between them, wearing the number 10 shirt carries with it so much prestige at all levels of the game, as quoted on azquotes.com

“I always want more. Whether it’s a goal, or winning a game, I’m never satisfied.”

LIONEL MESSI

The hunger of a born winner, stripped back for all to see… as quoted in Verve Magazine, *2016*

“Rest in peace, @Pele.”

LIONEL MESSI

Leo’s simple social media message after the passing of the Brazilian legend, 30 December 2022

“We competed individually and as a team for the same goals. It was a very beautiful stage for us and also for the people because they enjoyed it very much. It is a beautiful memory that will remain in the history of football.”

LIONEL MESSI

on Cristiano Ronaldo after the former Real Madrid striker's explosive interview with Piers Morgan, as quoted on mirror.co.uk, November 2022

“The only thing that matters is playing. I have enjoyed it since I was a little boy, and I still try to do that every time I go out on to a pitch. I always say that when I no longer enjoy it or it's no longer fun to do it, then I won't do it anymore. I do it because I love it and that's all I care about.”

LIONEL MESSI

speaking prior to the 2014 World Cup final, as quoted on reuters.com, July 2014

“I heard that so much, both before and after the World Cup. I felt people wanted me to win this. I can’t explain it, because there was never something like this, or at least I don’t remember anything like that. All that energy, and everyone wanting this, that’s what made this happen.”

LIONEL MESSI

in conversation with Argentine radio host Andy Kusnetzoff in January 2023, as quoted in the Buenos Aires Herald, *April 2023*

"I love playing football and while I feel like I'm in good shape and enjoying this, I'm going to keep at it."

LIONEL MESSI

Words we all want to hear! Leo admits he has no plans of hanging up his boots just yet, as quoted on givemesport.com, February 2023